The World
that Jack Built

For Dieter, Clara, Angela and Lilian

A Red Fox Book

Published by Random Century Children's Books, 20 Vauxhall Bridge Road, London SW1V 2SA.
A division of the Random Century Group

London Melbourne Sydney Auckland Johannesburg and agencies throughout the world

First published by Andersen Press Limited 1990

Red Fox edition 1991

© Ruth Brown

Printed and bound in Italy by Grafiche AZ, Verona

ISBN 0 09 978960 4

The World
that Jack Built

Ruth Brown

RED FOX

This is the house that Jack built.

These are the trees that grow by the house that Jack built.

This is the stream that flows past the trees, that grow by the house that Jack built.

These are the meadows which border the stream, which
flows past the trees, that grow by the house that Jack built.

These are the woods that shelter the meadows, that border the stream, which flows past the trees, that grow by the house that Jack built.

These are the hills which form the valley, that surrounds the woods, that shelter the meadows, which border the stream, that flows past the trees, that grow by the house that Jack built.

These are the hills that form the valley next to the one that protects the woods, that shelter the meadows, which border the stream, that flows past the trees, that grow by the house that Jack built.

And these are the woods which cover those hills –

and shelter the meadows —

which border the stream –

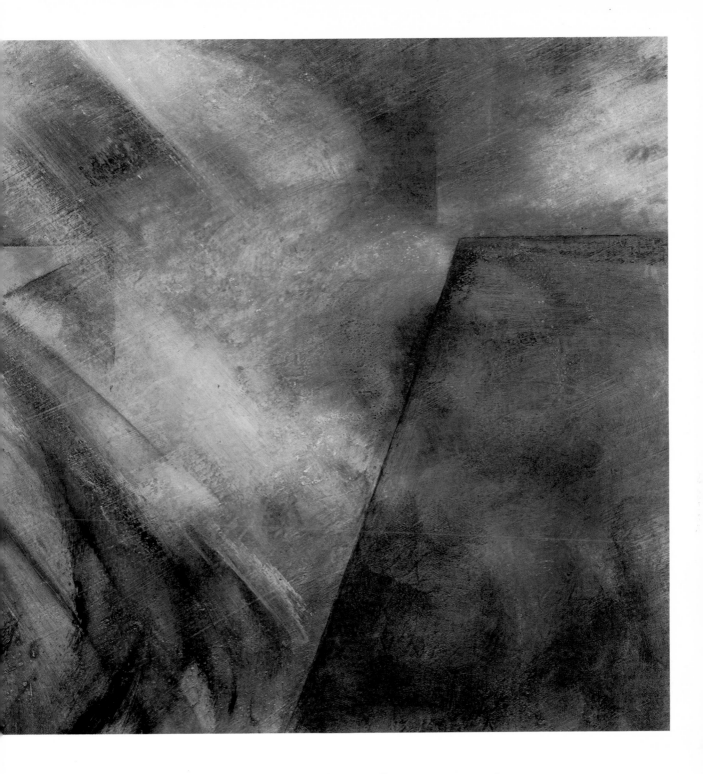

that flows past the place where the trees used to grow –

next to the factory that Jack built.

Other titles in the Red Fox picture book series (incorporating Beaver Books)